Also by Ivor Kenny

Industrial Democracy: Symposium Proceedings (1969)

The Atlantic Management Study

Government and Enterprise in Ireland (1984)

In Good Company: Conversations with Irish Leaders (1987)

*Out on Their Own: Conversations with Irish
Entrepreneurs (1991)*

Boardroom Practice

*Talking to Ourselves: Conversations with Editors of Irish
News Media (1994)*

The Death of Shibboleths

Freedom and Order: Studies in Strategic Leadership (1999)

Leaders: Conversations with Irish Chief Executives (2001)

Can You Manage? (2003)

*Achievers: Visionary Irish Leaders Who Achieved Their
Dreams (2005)*

Last Word: A Life Working with Managers (2006)

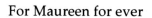

For Maureen for ever

And if the world were black or white entirely
And all the charts were plain
Instead of a mad weir of tigerish waters,
A prism of delight and pain,
We might be surer where we wished to go
Or again we might be merely
Bored but in brute reality there is no
Road that is right entirely.

Louis MacNeice

CONTENTS

Acknowledgements   xi

Introduction: What the Book is About   1

1. Are You Being Served?   3
2. The Market — The Alpha and Omega   7
3. In Praise of Ambiguity   12
4. On Having It Both Ways   15
5. Nobody Will Do What I Tell Them   18
6. Self-Control   21
7. Five Commandments of Leadership   24
8. Without Followers, There Can Be No Leaders   28
9. The Good John Smith and the Bad John Smith   31
10. Slow-Brewed   34
11. Two Kinds of People   37
12. Integrity   41
13. The Vision Thing   44
14. Strategy   47
15. The Fallacy of Compulsion   52
16. Opportunity is Bald Behind   55
17. Managing Change   57
18. Organisation Structure: A Classic Either/Or   61
19. How Do Managers Learn?   66
20. Unfinished Business   69
21. Afterthought: Briars and Brambles —
    Barriers to Truth   72

ACKNOWLEDGEMENTS

I am deeply indebted to the many managers I work with and from whom I continue to learn.

Two lifelong friends — Joe Gilmartin, a teacher, and the late Ray Curran, a CEO, sadly missed — read the manuscript and helped me avoid the grosser errors.

Gillian Acton, my friend and colleague in UCD, completed 15 years with me on the day the book was finished.

Ken Lee, the illustrator, is a pleasure to work with.

Brian O'Kane of Oak Tree Press is a supportive and tolerant publisher.

INTRODUCTION:
WHAT THE BOOK IS ABOUT

"You've written nine or 10 books", a friend said to me. "Any chance you could put them through a mangle and squeeze out some of the lessons you've learned? Put them in a *short* book a manager can read and think about on a transatlantic flight."

I have tried to distil into a slim volume lessons learned working with managers for 40 years — 20 in the Irish Management Institute, where I became familiar with theory, and 20 in UCD where I work with managers in international companies. I have plundered earlier books and added new material, about half-and-half.

Blaise Pascal said he was writing a long letter because he did not have time to write a short one. Boiling things down to fit that transatlantic flight was a useful exercise. At least it stopped me banging on, pounding points to death. But it can have the opposite danger of a *reductio ad absurdum*, where sharp points can be missed in a hasty read.

I have tried to strike a balance. Only the reader can judge. Striking a balance is the theme of the book.

Plundering my own work was a rediscovery of an enduring belief — that human imperfection is intractable. Human imperfection means that we are faced with the humble task of endless improvisation, where one good is compromised for the sake of others, where a price has to be paid for everything, where a *balance* is sought among the necessary conflicts of human life and disaster is staved off for another day.

Managers always face apparent opposites: sensitive *versus* macho management; short-term *versus* long-term; low-cost *versus* added-value; top-down *versus* bottom- up . . .

The point of the book is that, since few things are black and white, clear-cut, either/or, *we have to manage in a way that accepts the existence of contradictory phenomena without trying to resolve them.* This goes against the grain of a culture that would see managers as sturdy and determined. Obdurate? Rock-like obduracy won't get you very far in a world that is complex, changing and chaotic.

On the other hand, it is liberating to stop trying to reconcile the irreconcilable. It frees your mind of *idées fixes* and opens it to opportunities that, in pursuit of the impossible, you may have missed.

I believe that managers, when they get precious time to think, know this. Seasoned managers, who have faced failure, know it well. The book cannot be a finger-wagging exercise. Managers would not thank you for it. My hope is that it can be a reminder, timely or otherwise, that brings to the surface thoughts buried under the press of events.

Ivor Kenny
Dublin
December 2013

1
ARE YOU BEING SERVED?

Do you love your customers?
If you don't, you may be in the wrong job.

Have you ever battled your way on a dark evening into a crushed and crowded aircraft, to hear one stewardess say, audibly, to the other, "Growlers tonight"?

I stood at the reception desk of an Irish hotel vainly trying to check out while two flustered receptionists failed to cope. There was a medical conference on and a participant with "Doctor" emblazoned on his lapel badge asked politely to see the duty manager — his wife had food poisoning following the dinner the night before. A young man in black jacket and striped trousers arrived to tell the doctor that nobody else had complained.

Why is it that some businesses convey accurately the impression that they hate their customers?

On the other hand, some years ago I was driving with a friend through the leafy backroads of New York State to find the house of the futurologist, Herman Kahn. We were almost lost when we saw a policeman on a magnificent white motorbike. He gave us detailed instructions, saluted, and we drove off.

A few minutes later, I saw him in the rear-view mirror. I pulled over and he said, "I've decided my directions were too complicated. Follow me".

Recently, I got a bill from my garage. I had not been charged for a particularly expensive replacement part, even though the car was out of the guarantee period. When I queried the bill, I was told the item was so expensive they had decided not to charge me for it. They made a customer for life.

And, as we know, the purpose of a business is to create a customer.

My point is that it's difficult to create (or retain) customers if you don't love them. *Do you love your customers?* If you don't, you may be in the wrong job.

If deep down your attitude to your customers is exploitive, no matter what appears on the smooth surface, that attitude will be sensed and, with competition intensifying, your customers can go elsewhere.

While some things — unkept promises — are unforgivable, customers can be forgiving if their experience of your business is one of genuine concern for them.

I was chairman of a state company. I was invited to the Christmas party. The staff and their spouses coped with it in two ways. Either they sat in a circle on hard chairs, clutching their Club Oranges, noting everything and storing it for future use, or they arrived late with guilty grins.

Dinner was served. The first course was canned grapefruit segments served in one of those battered silver dishes. The second was humorously called soup. Then came the *pièce de résistance*, turkey and ham. I turned around to look at the oval serving dish. On it were little piles of paper-thin slices of turkey on paper-thin slices of ham, set on a suspicious substance which was, presumably, stuffing. The meat looked as if it had been carved at dawn. Every now and then someone in the kitchen had taken pity on it and poured gravy over. The marks of several receding tides were visible.

When I turned, my eyes met the waitress's: fiftyish, pure Dublin, tight blond hair, well-groomed, had seen it all, would not say "No" to a drop of gin. She murmured, "Yes sir, wouldn't it sicken you".

Those few words turned a disaster into an event.

While Mark McCormack said, "All things being equal, people will buy from a friend. All things being not quite so equal, people will still buy from a friend", I am not for a moment suggesting that we, the lovable Irish, should get away with murder. I am not advocating soft oul' *grá-mo-chroí* management. What I am saying is that, no matter how smooth and professional you are, it will not count for much if that professionalism is not imbued with a love of your customers. Delta Airlines' motto is: We love to fly and it shows.

But, antecedent to that love there is an even more important one, love of the work you do. If you don't love your job — *and* your product or service — you *can't* love your customers.

Do you go to work whistling or gloomy? Do you come home weary or with a sense of accomplishment?

When I am advising managers who may have lost their way I end up telling them they have three choices:

- Change the job from inside, i.e. bend and shape the job, if you can, more closely to coincide with what you like doing. This would require a fairly flexible and tolerant organisation — qualities for which most organisations are not noted.

- Two, change the job by getting out. This choice has dangers. You may carry your psychological baggage from one environment to another. On the other hand, you may have the courage really to change what you are doing, even if it means a loss of income or status.

- Three, have a problem.

And people who have a problem will take it out on their subordinates — and on their customers.

2
THE MARKET –
THE ALPHA AND OMEGA

Quality is a journey that never ends — you have to do
it every day.

In 1987, I conducted a study of the Gilbey's Group for David
Dand. As I stood in their great warehouse on the Naas Road and
looked at row upon row of cases of Baileys Irish Cream, stacked
to the roof, I thought of the thousands of individual customer
decisions to buy a single bottle of Baileys. If ever there was a
picture of the size of the market, this was it.

The market is where management begins — and ends. The
market is where distinctiveness is created — and eliminated.

Selling alcohol is the purest form of marketing. There are only
two reasons to drink alcohol: to get a bit jarred and, secondly,
because we like the taste. There is an infinite number of products
competing for our attention on both counts. Selling branded
vodka is the purest of all forms of marketing because it qualifies
on only the first count.

Marketing is the art of finding, developing and profiting from
opportunities. It is a pathfinder activity. David Dand (who died
too young) was a pathfinder. He was obsessed with quality.

In the duty free at Singapore airport, he saw a bottle of Baileys
with the label on crooked. He immediately phoned home and
read the riot act.

I was walking along a corridor in head office with him when
we met a young salesman who was wearing a beautifully cut

double-breasted blazer, dark flannels, a white shirt and sober tie. I thought he looked very smart. David said, "Murphy, are you going on a picnic?".

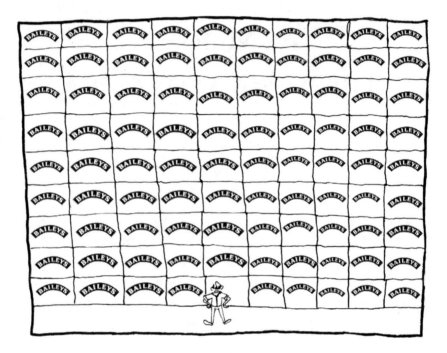

The best thing I can do is let David tell his own tale (from a conversation I recorded in 1990). It is not only the story of Ireland's leading branded product, and the largest-selling liqueur in the world, it is also a story of several of the leadership qualities we shall talk about later.

> We moved to the Naas Road in 1970 and that's really where the Baileys story begins. We had, of course, been manufacturing Smirnoff, a brand I had brought back from the States in 1961 when I was sent for a week to a Hublein conference and stayed a month. Vodka was not consumed in Ireland back in the early sixties and we were getting precisely nowhere with Gilbey's gin. I told the advertising agency that we were now going to spend on this marvellous new product all the money we had been spending trying for

the third time to resuscitate Gilbey's gin. They thought I was insane. Now vodka accounts for 23% of all the spirits sold in Ireland.

I've worked on gut feel, on intuition, rather than on any scientific assessment of what is right or wrong.

We used to have these brain-storming meetings and we decided emphatically that, if we were going to grow and expand the business, we had to get into exporting. We tried several mixtures, an imitation vermouth, an Irish sherry — but none of these was going to be primarily sourced in Ireland. That's how Irish cream and Irish whiskey came together. We had some research done and we found that chocolate was one of the most popular flavours in the world. And we put those three things together — literally with a Kenwood mixer. It tasted delicious.

We went to I.D.V's (our parent company's) technical people in Harlow. They said that it was a bloody good idea but that it could not be done. I said that it was such a good idea that we must do it, putting on my hat of not taking "No" for an answer. It took them four years before we got a product that was sufficiently good to put on the market and, even then, it was not great. We launched on November 26, 1974 in Dublin only and we started exporting in 1975. We built it market by market and the great thing about it was that it has been a profitable business since day one. Since then, we have spent £40m here in Dublin on capital equipment. We are exporting to every country in the world that is able to import and sell alcoholic beverages.

When I go through immigration and the official asks me what business I'm in, I say, "Liquor". They then always ask, "What kind of liquor?" And I say, "Baileys" and they always instantly recognise it – it's fantastic.

Vodka is a neutral spirit and, in many ways, is the very essence of branding. In branding, the consumer has to perceive added value, a value that distinguishes the product from other similar ones. The two things have to be there: both the perception and the intrinsic quality. You have to pack perceived added value with quality. You can't cod people. Quality is a journey that never ends. You can never say we've got it right — you have to do it every day.

If you don't believe in the brand yourself, there is no way you can persuade your customers that the brand will sell. If you have any doubts in your mind about the brand, sure as hell those doubts will show. If you do believe in the brand, then that belief comes across naturally. I deeply believed in the product from day one and increasingly as it proved relatively easy to sell. You have to do it yourself before you can transmit that belief. The second thing was to get a team of people around me. Now I have appointed Ned Sullivan as managing director of Baileys to take over the job I held.

You ask me if it was hard to let that job go. The answer is no, not at all, when you find a brilliant marketeer like Ned Sullivan. He is also more technically qualified in marketing than I am. I would call myself a marketing entrepreneur rather than a university-qualified (which I am not) marketing pro. Ned is the true professional. There are things that Ned can do that I can't do and — just possibly — there are things that I can do that perhaps Ned could not do.

No one should think in terms of life cycles for brands. In the early days the comment was made that Baileys was a here-today-gone-tomorrow, that the taste was so delicious that people were going to get fed up with it.

What you've got to do with brands — both with Baileys, which is tasteful, and with Smirnoff, which is tasteless — is to keep recycling them.

Brands are not like people — they don't die naturally. They die from neglect. When you see fashions or demographics changing, you must change your direction. We do this with Baileys all the time. We are having workshops, we are consulting, we are talking with our agents from overseas, keeping our eyes and ears open to changes in the marketplace.

And selling is terribly important. I always say to the guys, "You should treat the next bottle like the first bottle you ever sold". If you do that your brand will always be new, it will always be live.

3

IN PRAISE OF AMBIGUITY

Macho managers go like a bull at a gate.
The better manager is adept at handling complexity.

As David Dand's story illustrates, management is practice. There are few blueprints, few grand plans. There are no solutions that can be transferred shrink-wrapped from one piece of experience to another. That is not to say that nothing is fixed, that there are no guidelines, that we can make everything up as we go along.

It is to say that correction is contingent on the constraints and opportunities of the time, the culture or sedimented attitudes of the people we have to work with.

That benign philosopher, E.F. Schumacher, who first said, "Small is beautiful", wrote,

> *Some people always tend to clamour for a final solution, as if in life there could ever be a final solution other than death. For constructive work, the principal task is always the restoration of some kind of balance.*

And, as *The Book of Common Prayer* says, we should avoid "the two extremes, of too much stiffness in refusing, and too much easiness in admitting any variation".

Management is always about balance, about freedom *and* order.

Balance means the acceptance of paradox.

Some years ago I brought the French and Irish board members of the Smurfit Paribas Bank off for a day to answer the question, "What kind of bank do you want?"

On one flipchart, we wrote words like: warm, friendly, welcoming, relaxed, non-hierarchical. On another we wrote: entrepreneurial, quick-moving, decisive and so on. Which did they choose? Both.

Poulsen[1] has presented a list of paradoxes:

- To be able to build a close relationship with your staff . . . *and to keep a subtle distance.*

- To be able to lead . . . *and to hold yourself in the background.*

- To trust your staff . . . *and to keep an eye on what is happening.*

- To be tolerant . . . *and to know how you want things to function.*

- To keep the goals of your own department in mind . . . *and at the same time to be loyal to the whole firm.*

- To do a good job of planning your own time . . . *and to be flexible with your schedule.*

- To express your own views freely . . . *and to be diplomatic.*

- To be a visionary . . . *and to keep your feet on the ground.*

- To try to win consensus . . . *and to be able to cut through.*

- To be dynamic . . . *and to be reflective.*

- To be sure of yourself . . . *and to be humble.*

Michael Smurfit said, "*Logical opportunism* means being creative while keeping a strong grip on the key day-to-day elements of the business". Logic (thought) and opportunism (action) are not opposites. We need the "Let's go!" of leadership. We also need the "Hold on a minute" of cool advice. Just as we need both patience and impatience.

Ambiguity (*ambi-*, both ways; *agere*, to drive) has two important things to offer managers. First, it is useful in thinking about how we communicate with others. Second, it provides a

---

[1] P. Thygesen Poulsen (1993), "The Paradoxes of Success", LEGO – en virksomhead og dens sjael, Copenhagen: Schultz.

way of legitimising the loose rein that a manager permits in situations where agreement needs time, or where more insight is needed before decisive action can be taken.

Many managers are under fierce day-to-day pressure merely to survive. Macho managers go like a bull at a gate. They may succeed once. The second time, the gate has been reinforced and all they get is a sore head. The better manager is adept at handling complexity and its consequent ambiguity.

4

ON HAVING IT BOTH WAYS

Avoid using a sledgehammer when a feather will do.
But keep the hammer handy.

Our drive for the explicit stems from the notion that it's a matter of honour to get all the cards out on the table. There is also the notion that, no matter how much it hurts, full frontal exposure is good for you: the sign of a good manager is his or her ability to give and take negative feedback.

No doubt there is merit in this conventional wisdom. But the true state of things often lies between the mythology of our management lore and our human foibles. It is good to get the facts and to know where you stand. But it's also human to feel threatened when you are vulnerable.

Proclaiming the need to "speak the truth" often unmasks a self-serving sense of brute integrity. "Clearing the air" can be more helpful to the clearer than to those starkly revealed. It is not just an outcome of a certain cultural tendency to speak bluntly. Simplistic confrontation — a *High Noon* shoot-out — is mixed up with notions of strength. Shoot-outs work best when the other guy dies. When you have to continue to work with him, such macho confrontations complicate life: he will be waiting in the long grass.

By contrast, the ambiguity that stems from sensitivity to people's feelings may be seen as weakness. But sensitivity does not rule out toughness when toughness is needed. It does not mean taking the easy way out — the corruption of management. It does not mean that there will never be confrontations best dealt with by the effective use of two syllables. But we should not confuse heroics with effectiveness. Are brute integrity and explicit communication worth the price of the listener's trust, goodwill, open-mindedness and receptivity to change?

Management by decree has a part to play in organisations, particularly in emergencies. But, more often than not, a sudden lurch to a new order will evoke resistance that works with enduring effectiveness.

Our notions of leadership are sometimes confined to a number of images: strength, firmness, determination and clarity of vision. We like to think of leaders as lonely figures capable of decisive action in the face of adversity. These assumptions — for that is what they are — can act as fortresses, keeping other important things out of our awareness.

Approaching things purposively, defining problems crisply and identifying explicitly our objectives are desirable, but not necessarily sufficient, qualities with which to manage all problems skillfully. We might also bear in mind that a macho view of the world lessens our sensitivity and skills. Such an insight may enable us to avoid using a sledgehammer when a feather will do. But keep the hammer handy.

5

NOBODY WILL DO
WHAT I TELL THEM

There is nothing more frightening than ignorance in motion.

Many years ago I was on a lecture tour of India. At the end of the tour, when I was very tired, I was conducting a seminar for chief executives in a small hot room in what was then called Bombay with geckos climbing up the green distempered walls. An extremely wealthy Indian gentleman had come with his son to learn from the Irish guru. He kept shaking his head in the Indian fashion to indicate agreement.

I said, "Mr. Patel, you are agreeing with me?"

"Yes, yes, Mr. Kenny, I am agreeing with you."

I said, somewhat wearily, "Mr. Patel, what are you agreeing with?".

He said, "What my company needs is more human relations".

I said, "Mr. Patel, what do you mean by human relations?".

He said, "Nobody will do what I tell them".

You must have some sympathy for Mr. Patel. He *founded* the company. He led it from small beginnings through several near-failures to many successes. He *owned* the company, dammit. And these people to whom he gave their livelihood would not do what he told them.

(In India, incidentally, the workers had an effective ultimate sanction, a *gherao*. They would surround the bosses and not let them out until they capitulated: a kind of lock-in rather than a lock-out.)

Mr. Patel was finding for himself what Peter Drucker wrote in *The Age of Discontinuity*: "Management is simple but not easy. The simple part is knowing what to do. The part that is not easy is getting others to do it.".

At every airport, there are books that subtract from the sum of human knowledge by reducing to a number of simple slogans the complex job of managing. Slogans stir the blood when they confirm our prejudices. They are then a sure barrier to learning — because we *think* we know.

Anyone who can complete in a phrase the sentence, "What this company (or country) needs is . . ." is bound to be wrong.

Let's look at some of the phrases managers use to avoid complexity:

- JFDI (just ... do it).
- Let's get on with the job.
- Keep your eye on the ball.
- All that matters is the bottom line.
- It's time they realised which side their bread is buttered on.
- The only thing they understand is . . .
- What would you expect of . . .?

No one expects managers to be philosophers — but, on the other hand, the impulse to instant activity, the reduction of complexity to childish slogans, the "let-me-have-it-on-one-sheet-of-paper" syndrome, can suppress the reality of the world and lead to surprises, many of them unpleasant. There is nothing more frightening than ignorance in motion.

In one of Mervyn Wall's books, the sergeant is having a quiet pint. It's past closing time. The blinds are down and the door locked. The sergeant slowly turns from the counter. Silence falls. The locals sense he is about to make a statement.

He says, "I think Stalin has something up his sleeve".

6
SELF-CONTROL

*True humility is knowing yourself and the effects of
your actions on others.*

There is not much use in having high leadership skills if you don't
really know what's going on in your organisation. At Henley
Royal Regatta, there is a phenomenon known as "tap point". Late
in the summer evening, the old, old Leander man, his wattles
empurpled with port, which he drinks from a tankard, is tapping
his companion on the lapel of his ancient blazer and harping, "But
you're not listening to what I'm saying". Let's look at some
reasons why leaders may reach tap point.

Walter Lippman said: "The very rarest of princes can endure
even a little criticism, and few of them can put up with even a
pause in adulation".

Tony O'Reilly said: "I am less effective when I am angry and
irritated. I am not as eloquent, not as thoughtful, and I'm often
wrong".

O'Reilly is talking about humility — not the false abasement of
a Uriah Heep, but the humility of knowing yourself and of the
effects of your actions on others.

Lippman is talking about the corruption of leadership, where
narcissism has replaced self-knowledge, where applause replaces
reality.

I have never met a chief executive who had got that bad. But
many chief executives have a vision and the suggestion that
unpleasant events may attend its pursuit can be viewed as an
attack. No company can afford such conceit for long.

Very few of us are good listeners. We half-hear what the other person is saying and wholly-hear what's going on inside our own heads. Among the first signs of the corruption of leadership is a leader who has stopped listening. He may attribute his high success to his unique personal qualities. He may begin to resent criticism, particularly when he hears it from lesser mortals who, he believes, have nothing approaching his experience and ability. He may become less tolerant and evince impatience and petulance — and will surely choke off essential channels of information, causing in his subordinates fear, dependency and dishonesty.

The reason for his behaviour may be that, in Lord Acton's words, power itself has corrupted him (or, in our own words, that he has lost the run of himself).

More often than not, however, he is merely passing on to his subordinates his own anxieties. Anxieties spread like ink on blotting paper.

A chief executive has considerable clout. Any time I have said that to a chief executive, I have got a wan look and a "You must be joking". The greater part of a chief executive's life is spent removing obstacles. When he looks out on the world he sees an awful lot of things he can't do. When a subordinate looks up at him he sees an awful lot of power.

If a chief executive's board is baying for bottom-line blood, it would take heroic virtue not to let some of that pressure spill over on to subordinates. It is the way it spills that is important.

7

FIVE COMMANDMENTS OF LEADERSHIP

A leader who has sorted out his inner conflicts will convey a sense of optimism and hope.

The beginning of control is self-control. The effective leader has his own house in order. He is able to resolve inner conflicts so that, for example, he does not, because of his own mixed feelings, constantly make decisions and then undo them to the confusion of his subordinates.

If a leader is immobilised in the face of a difficult problem, he may look outside himself to explain why. This is *projection*. A person projects when, unknown to himself, he takes an attitude of his own and attributes it to someone else. The leader who despairs because his subordinates are confused and indecisive may well be reading his own state of mind and attributing it to them.

When the leader is able to identify and to separate what he feels within himself from what is happening around him, power struggles and rivalries within the organisation are more easily understood and more subject to rational control. It is easier to control and change yourself than to control and change the world.

The effective leader knows that he does not have to win every argument. Management requires a give-and-take where it is impossible for everyone to be right all the time. Giving way to a compelling argument is no loss of face.

The leader who can develop a position, believe in it, support it to its fullest and then back down when he is shown a better way, is a strong person. Humility is a virtue.

But we should not equate that virtue with behaviour that *appears* modest, uncertain of a stand and acquiescent towards others — behaviour which anyway is likely to be feigned. True humility is a mark of the person who thinks his way through problems, is willing to be assertive, encourages assertiveness in others and can acknowledge ideas better than his own.

The five commandments of self-control are well known.

The first is to understand your own motivations. Here you will probably need outside help — a wise and trusted adviser with whom you can be utterly frank and who won't let you kid yourself. You can't control your actions and responses until you understand their well-springs. We are possessed of the cardinal virtues: prudence, justice, fortitude and temperance. But the penny catechism reminded us also that original sin darkened our understanding, weakened our will and left in us a strong inclination to evil.

It would be nice if we were always nice. We are not. As well as being possessed of virtues, we are possessed of a dark underworld of passions and instincts. We can deal effectively with situations in the degree to which we understand our own reactions to them. Give thy thoughts no tongue nor any unproportion'd thought his act.

Second, remember what was written on the temple at Delphi: Know thyself. Leadership requires that you know who you are and who you are not. Being an all-round guy is pathetic. Trying to be someone else, some role model or mythical character, is worse.

Third, this above all: To thine own self be true, and it must follow, as the night the day, thou canst not then be false to any man. Having established who you are and who you are not, be consistent. Mood swings are confusing. They are particularly upsetting to subordinates who are entitled to the sense of security that comes from their boss's inner security. Flying off the handle, going ballistic, is not only self-indulgent, it causes a profound loss of respect.

Fourth, identify and concentrate on a limited number of significant issues. No matter how skilful the leader is in focusing his energies, he gets caught up in a number of inconsequential things. They can drain emotional energy. Say "No" without the feeling that you have lost esteem. The ability to say no shows you do not need esteem to bolster a flagging ego.

Fifth, learn to communicate. The old saw about having two ears and one mouth is worth repeating to yourself. Be aware of your own reactions (as we said). And try to make known your opinions and attitudes without delay. If they are left to simmer they will probably boil over at the wrong time.

There is a Yiddish saying: "If somebody tells you you have ears like a donkey, pay no attention. If two people tell you, buy yourself a saddle."

Shut up and listen.

And remember the story of the little boy who sat on the pavement in the Ramblas in Barcelona, his cup held out for coins, his big brown eyes full of tears. The passers-by passed him by. An old beggar came along and said, "You must not look sad. You must smile and be happy and make the passers-by happy". That's what the little boy did — and his cup overflowed.

Nobody will follow a gloomy leader for long. A leader who has sorted out his inner conflicts will convey a sense of optimism and hope.

Cheer up.

8

WITHOUT FOLLOWERS, THERE CAN BE NO LEADERS

Leadership is a combination of character (who you are) and competence (what you can do).

A leader is someone who has willing followers. Without followers, there can be no leaders. Leadership is a combination of character (who you are) and competence (what you can do). Leaders carry the ultimate responsibility. They are personally accountable for *results*, for deeds not words.

Most managers operate within existing ways of thinking. Leaders challenge those ways — they are happiest when they are changing things. They are seldom content. They never arrive. There is always another mountain to climb.

And they are all different.

Among the most effective leaders I have worked with over 40 years, some were gregarious, enjoying people and parties; others were solitary, preferring the sanctuary of their families. Some were nice guys; others were affectionately known as right bastards. Some were impulsive and moved too quickly; others took ages to decide. Some were warm and welcoming; others were distant and aloof. Some were vain and sought publicity; for others publicity was pointless — the chairman and CEO of one major company would not go to the AGM. Some were austere — a decent suit and a modest car — others were ostentatious to the point of vulgarity. Some sought adulation; others would be embarrassed by it. Some were introvert and, having listened to advice, would work things out inside their heads; others were extrovert, thinking aloud and changing their minds as the discussion progressed.

The one thing several of them did *not* have was charisma.

I have come to the conclusion that charisma does not matter a damn. If you have it, it can be helpful for getting attention, but it can also be showbiz, self-indulgent and overpowering, inhibiting genuine communication.

I'm almost minded to start an Anti-Charismatic Movement. I am not suggesting that business schools should run courses on How to be Dull and Boring — we can manage that without help — but there is a certain obsession with celebrity and charisma.

The line between fame and notoriety is unclear. We are confronted with a jumble of celebrities: the talented and untalented, heroes and villains, people of accomplishment and those who have accomplished nothing at all. The criterion for their celebrity is that their images give enough of the *appearance* of leadership — wealth, success, glamour and excitement — to feed our fantasies. Failure to question the qualifications of people to be celebrated is perverse — for we are who we celebrate.

The charismatic leader's style can be superficially attractive. But charismatic leaders are unreliable. You do not know until the final act what their real purposes are. Perhaps they do not know themselves. I revisited *Brideshead* recently and came across this: "Charm is the great English blight. It does not exist outside these damp islands. It spots and kills anything it touches. It kills love, it kills art.". Charisma and charm could well be synonyms.

In uncertain times, we look for a magician, a heroic figure. We look for a rainmaker. We get no rain. A constant threat is that people listen to the charismatic leader. Charismatic leadership is to be deeply distrusted: the man with the mad and unblinking eyes. In extremes, a group will give power to its most paranoid member. Only he or she can articulate their unconscious fears.

However, we are finding increasingly that "leaders" in Church and State have feet of clay. That is part of growing up: of maturing into a less dependent, less deferential and, hopefully, more responsible society.

Once it was "Follow me". Now we are a negotiating society. If we are to apply new solutions to new problems, we shall have to part with some received ideas about authority and hierarchy. That does not mean that leaders have to become one of the boys. Leaders who court popularity cut forlorn figures. And that is not what their followers expect of them.

Warren Bennis has written: "Books on leadership are often as majestically useless as they are pretentious". (That did not stop him writing many many books about it.)

Chester Barnard said, "Leadership has been the subject of an extraordinary amount of dogmatically stated nonsense". Barnard was echoed in a recent hilarious study by Micklethwait and Wooldridge: "Within the wayward word-spattering world of management theory, no subject has produced more waffle than leadership. By one count, there are 130 different definitions . . .".

9

THE GOOD JOHN SMITH
AND THE BAD JOHN SMITH

*Leaders have passed their life-cycle when they continue
to apply old remedies to new situations.*

Much of the literature on leadership gives a top-down view. The
work I do gives a bottom-up, a follower's, view.

Let's call those leaders I worked with the Good John Smith and
the Bad John Smith. This is what their *followers* thought of them.

The good John Smith is seen by his subordinates as an
inspiring leader, dedicated, likeable, a big loss if he left. He takes
the long view. He is accessible and supportive, stays in touch. He
lets you get on with it, but looks for results. He has integrity and
is decisive. He knows the business but may have to change as it
changes.

The bad John Smith is dominant and autocratic. He tends to
decide everything. He is remote, aloof, does not tell people what's
going on. He, in turn, is not told the truth. His style encourages
sycophancy and dependency. He encourages cronyism. He can be
inconsistent, moody and emotional. He shows little appreciation.

The important thing is that the Good John Smith and the Bad
John Smith are not two people. Like Jekyll and Hyde, they are
different aspects of one and the same person.

What we have is a picture of perceived individual behaviour. It
is also a picture of a relationship. That relationship is like an
electric cable. It contains a warm positive wire and a cold negative
one. Which is in the ascendant can depend on circumstances: the
smile of appreciation, the frown of humiliation — he is a bad

bastard, or, he's not such a bad bastard after all. The good John Smith and the bad John Smith do not necessarily cancel out each other. In their duality, they represent the human condition.

Danger can come when leaders are seen to have passed their product life-cycle, when they continue to apply old remedies to new situations. The best know this and depart.

What may pass for wisdom and experience can be a crippling disability, when only a rejection of the past can secure the future.

St. Paul, following St. Matthew, said, "If any among you think himself wise in this world, let him become a fool that he may be wise".

It may be in becoming as little children (or as fools) that we are able to shake off the fetters of predisposing mental sets or to cast out any library of antiquated routines that block our access to the present. This may be the cathartic quality that we need first to command within ourselves if we are to command the changing society in which we work.

Before a new Pope is enthroned, a friar stands in front of him and lights a piece of hempen rope which flares and goes out. This is to remind the Pope of the vanities of leadership. Mediaeval monarchs employed a court jester who could say in jest what the courtiers could not say in seriousness.

10

SLOW-BREWED

The most common description of good bosses is "Tough but fair".

A cynic might say to me that there are only two questions I need ask of the managers when I enter an organisation: "How long have you been here?" and "What harm has it done you?". Leaders and their organisations can do bad things to people.

A better question to ask is, "How many bosses have you had in your working life?". Some managers turn out to have had many. Then I ask, "Which ones do you recall with gratitude and affection as really good?". The most I ever get is one or two; at any rate, a tiny minority of the whole. Last, I ask them to describe those good bosses.

By far the most common description is "Tough but fair". That is not a scientific formulation. The important thing is that everybody seems to recognise it. Nobody says, "Fair but tough", or even, "Tough and fair". Tough comes first, expressed as a necessity, then fair. You have to be tough, but the toughness is OK if it is fair as well.

People who are remembered as "good" bosses have a certain kind of intelligence, a particular way of thinking that makes them memorable.

Their virtue is that they do not consciously exercise charismatic influence. They simply keep their eye on the ball, with a certain humility, but nonetheless grow in the fullness of time to have *earned* respect and influence.

Leadership is a quality of character and intellect, not a condition or empty honour. The indispensable ingredients are the ability:

- To sense the future[2]
- To understand the aspirations of followers
- To discern the limits of possibilities
- To select the lines of advance that hold the best promise of success.

Leaders are judged not by tactical nimbleness but by the robustness of their strategic designs. Good designs will be new, because they must contend with new circumstances. Any successful organisation is a monument to old problems successfully solved. Its very existence is proof of a good design in the past. But unchanging behaviour in rapidly changing conditions can cause a leader to look like a tree on a windswept heath. Those who can't change their minds, can't change anything. Hard-headed men who have made their perilous ascents to leadership have unbounded faith in their own beliefs, but those of them who change things penetrate the surface of events and break through inherited rigidities. Leaders barren of ideas are caretakers. Ideas uncoupled to the will, passion and skills of leaders are intellectual toys.

We do not know it all and we never can. But we know enough to answer the silly question: are leaders born or made?

It was Dean Inge, not Oscar Wilde, who said, "Nothing fails like success". One bit of experience essential to becoming a leader is failure. That is where there is real learning.

There is a sign hanging in Joe McHugh's pub in Liscannor, Co. Clare:

Experience is what you get when you didn't get what you wanted.

---

[2]   The words are Denis Brosnan's, Chairman and founding CEO of the Kerry Group, the most impressive strategist I have worked with.

Leaders are not born full-blown. Neither are they made like instant coffee. They are slow-brewed in the circumstances of the time.

11

TWO KINDS OF PEOPLE

*There are two discernible kinds of people and one of
them is disastrous in a position of power.*

We have all heard the joke that there are two kinds of people:
those who think there are two kinds of people and those who
don't. I really do believe there are two kinds of people in this
world, builders and pirates, and pirates ought never be promoted
to high rank — a gross generalisation, I know, but a useful one.

Most of us have no difficulty in determining who we like, who
we trust, and who we approve of. There ought to be a high
concurrence between those three judgments, yet we are too often
content to give leadership to people we would rather not invite
into our own homes.

It is not that we are taken in by the pirates. Perhaps it is
because we sometimes think of business as a kind of badland and
business leadership as demanding piratical instincts such as those
sensitively expressed by the late Mayor Curley of Boston: "Do
unto others what they would do unto you if they got the chance,
only do it first".

Pirates live their lives in single dimensions with work divorced
from personal values, from family, from leisure, from social
obligations. Their work is often at odds with what they personally
need.

This splitting of their job from all other aspects of their life
shows itself in rigidity, selfishness and hostility. The hostility is
unconscious and usually well disguised.

Builders see their work as giving purpose and significance to their whole lives. Their work is congruent with their personal needs. They do not make worse the historic conflict between personal and organisational needs. Why? Because they do not have the hostility that comes from the sycophantic way the pirate operates.

Sycophants feel they must agree with their boss to get ahead and, in hiding their true feelings, build up hostility against both the boss and the company. The organisation, in turn, invites subservience: subservience is easier to manage.

Pirates evaluate themselves quantitatively: by how much money they make; by how much power they have; by what car they drive; by what kind of house they live in; even, eventually, by what kind of friends they have.

Builders evaluate their work qualitatively. They think of personal growth rather than hierarchical status. They see social responsibility not as part of a job description but as part of their humanity. Because the measures are more qualitative, builders understand more than pirates do. They may be less effective, perhaps, in terms of the organisation's short-term goals — because of lack of concern for immediate results — but they are more valuable to the organisation's long-term flexibility and, therefore, survival.

Success for pirates is always empty. They reach the top of the ladder and they can only go down. Since they have been one-dimensional, all aspects of their lives decline. Fame lacks intimacy — hence the loneliness. We are then stuck with an obsolete person. Obsolete people have nothing to fall back on.

For the builders, success is continually experienced. Their fate is not decline — it is unfinished experience. The core dimension of their lives remains. They are constantly useful. They do not become embittered or sycophantic. They remain a healthy asset.

My argument so far is simple. There are two discernible kinds of people, and one of them is disastrous in a position of power. Piracy, however, in parallel with being disastrous, is likely to lead to *career* success and thus to a gross contribution to organisation inefficiency and madness, until, too late, the pirate is found out.

And pirates, often some of the most conventionally successful people, are emotional cripples doomed to spend most of their lives in a survival mode, unaware of the costs of their skewed psychology.

However, when it comes to deciding about who to select for leadership, the problem lies less in our recognition of these psychological types than in our distorted view of what is good for the organisation. We sometimes select people we can't stand because of a misguided belief that a certain kind of driven madness will impel the organisation in a sensible direction. We home in on the impulsion and neglect the direction, like the Ferrari owner with a faulty map who gets more quickly to the wrong place.

Objectively, there is not a great problem in the identification of pirates for what they are. We don't usually mistake awful people for nice ones or *vice versa*. But we make allowances for certain kinds of awfulness on the erroneous assumption that benefits may flow from peculiar gifts. This is unwise. Awful people are always a disaster in the end, though the more cunning they are (very cunning, as a rule), the more likely it is that their tracks will be covered by confusion or their guilt projected on to others less quick on their feet.

There may be hope in the words of the French essayist, Jean de la Bruyère: "Men fall from great fortune because of the same shortcomings that led to their rise". But it is cold comfort to know that flawed leaders will eventually self-destruct, because, in a fast-changing world, we don't have that much time.

12

INTEGRITY

Integrity is to be what you are.

I listened to a young chief executive talking with his colleagues. He quoted Samuel Johnson: "Integrity without knowledge is weak and useless — but knowledge without integrity is dangerous and dreadful".

Chambers defines integrity as wholeness, the unimpaired state of anything, uprightness, honesty.

Proverbs says: "Better is the poor man that walketh in his integrity, than he that is perverse in his lips . . .".

You have come out of meetings, turned to a colleague and asked, "What was all that about?" Or remember Ralph Waldo Emerson, "What you are shouts so loud, I can't hear what you say". (He also wrote, "The louder he talked of his honour, the faster we counted the spoons".)

Integrity has to do with truth, with reality. It is not what you would *like* things to be, what you would *want* things to be, what you might *think* things are. Integrity is about consistency, constancy. Integrity is to shoot the way one shouts. Integrity is plain dealing. Integrity is to walk naked, not to be encased in badges of office or authority. Integrity is to be *what you are*.

Managers may bring with them the attitudes, prejudices and narrow vertical skills of a different generation. They may feel that, having arrived, they have learned all they need to. The truth is that the time to start learning most seriously is when leadership is thrust upon you. Leaders are the ones who can cause the greatest harm. The most important lesson leaders may have to learn is how to forget, how to recognise when their own ingrained perceptions and knowledge become obsolete. This is Charles Handy's forgetting curve, the mirror image of the learning curve.

And IQ isn't everything. A brilliant academic record cannot ensure success in life or in management. First, people with a high IQ don't necessarily make good decisions — otherwise we'd all be hiring mathematicians. Second, people with a high IQ often fall into the intelligence trap, intellectualising their wrong decisions. Third, people with a high IQ are often so talented at arguing with and criticising others that they focus on that rather than on arriving at constructive solutions. An ounce of emotion can be more effective than a ton of facts.

A high IQ can be trumped by a high EQ — emotional intelligence. It consists, as we have been saying, of getting to know your own emotions, learning to manage those emotions, and learning to recognise and deal with the emotions of others. EQ cannot always be learned but it can be developed. Ask yourself honestly how well you react to the concerns of others. You bring your emotions to work with you.[3]

Bertie Ramsbottom:

> *But decisions, my friend,*
> *Are the means, not the end,*
> *And it's "how" more than "what" that may matter;*
> *So the wise are as ever,*
> *More rare than the clever —*
> *For there's more to decisions than data!*

Most of us have met the individual who believes he possesses the truth. He pursues highly simplified goals at the expense of thoughtful, open-minded, and compassionate concern for dissent and qualification. He offers the illusion of authority, a triumphant conviction of knowing his own mind when others appear to be wavering. In uncertain times, he can be an attractive figure until, inevitably, his certainty crumbles. He is dangerous.

We might heed the cautionary tale of the country doctor, a kindly man revered by his patients, but jealous also of his unquestioned authority.

A patient came to him in some distress. The doctor gave him as thorough an examination as his modest surgery allowed. At the end of it, the doctor did not have a clue what was wrong, but, unwilling to show any chink in his armour, asked the patient, "Have you had this before?" "I have, doctor". "Well, you have it again", said the doctor.

---

[3]   See Manfred Kets de Vries (2001), *The Leadership Mystique*, Edinburgh: Financial Times/Prentice Hall (*Recommended*: ISBN 0 273 65620 1)

13

THE VISION THING

The creative tension between what could be *and*
what is *constitutes a fundamentally different
approach to a strategic process.*

If chief executives are to live in any comfort they must foster an atmosphere in which their *vision*, their unique ideas, are continually understood and reinforced.

The longer I work with managers, the more I am impressed with our inability to forecast the future. For a year ahead, the headlamps can pick out some forms. After that it's darkness.

The theories of chaos and complexity are revealing the future as fundamentally unpredictable. This applies to the economy, to the stock market, to commodity prices, to the weather. There are no clear historical patterns that carve well-marked tracks into the future. History does not repeat itself. The future remains mostly unknowable. The Nobel prize-winner, Niels Bohr (not Groucho Marx), said, "Prediction is very difficult, especially about the future".

Winston Churchill complained that the future was one damned thing after another. Benjamin Franklin said the only things certain in life were death and taxes.

And our old friend Peter Drucker wrote, "Forecasting is not a respectable human activity and not worthwhile beyond the shortest of periods".

William A. Sherden told us about Paul Ehrlich, a professor of demography at Stanford University.[4] In 1968, Ehrlich wrote *The Population Bomb*, in which he predicted that, by the 1990s, war and pestilence, and possibly famine, would do us in. He said, "The most intelligent creatures ultimately surviving this period are cockroaches". Scary stuff.

Boston Globe columnist, Jeff Jacoby, called Ehrlich "the nation's most shameless fear monger, who has been richly rewarded for his almost perfect record of getting things wrong".

Herman Kahn forecast at an Irish Management Institute conference in Killarney that oil would never exceed $8 a barrel.

The future can look so uncertain that the only posture from which to confront it would seem to be on our knees.[5] If the future is unknowable, what then about vision, what about strategy?

---

[4] *The Fortune Sellers* (1998), New York: John Wiley.

[5] To help us get off our knees, read Peter Drucker, *Managing the Next Society* (2002), Oxford: Butterworth (*Highly recommended*: ISBN 0 7506 5624 7).

Vision is not so much a picture of an unknowable future as a statement of the values underlying an effective organisation.

What we need to do is to generate *a continuing creative tension between present reality and an articulated vision.*

Analysis will never generate a vision. To believe that strategic change can come about as a result of analysis is to fall into a reigning error: thinking we had solved a problem because we had described it. Failure is caused by substituting analysis for vision, in the belief that, if only people understood current reality, they would surely feel the motivation to change.

Here I have a confession to make because I once believed that too: that people are stimulated to change when confronted with the situation as it is. My work can make the need for change starkly apparent. It can reveal people's dissatisfaction. But it is not enough. Looking back over the many studies I have conducted, the ones that worked really well were those where there was a strong and decisive leader who could articulate a clear vision. The energy for change comes not from analysis alone, but from holding up a picture of *what could be* that is more desirable than *what is.* By changing a company's vision of itself, new energy is set free.

The creative tension between *what could be* and *what is* constitutes a fundamentally different approach to a strategic process: one in which forecasting still has a role to play, but where what we are forecasting is not just demand or sales, but rather those skills, capabilities, attitudes and resources required to compete successfully in the future.

The strategic challenge is to build an enduring arsenal of those essential skills and capabilities.

14
STRATEGY

Strategy is the step-by-step removal of removable constraints. Competitive strategy means deliberately choosing a different set of activities to deliver a unique mix of value.

Focusing on what we want to be has also a more subtle benefit. It lifts managers' eyes beyond the horizon, away from the multitude of grinding day-to-day problems. If a strategic discussion begins (and usually ends) with present reality, all you get is a cocktail of disagreement that can degenerate into blame-laying. Looking beyond the present to the kind of organisation we would like to be, can, if well led, be an optimistic and cheerful exercise.

Strategy, thus described, gives managers a *context* for decision-making and allocation of resources that leads to a clear purpose and competitive advantage. Strategy should not be developed because it is "the right thing to do" or because a silver-tongued consultant sells a ready-made process. Without the vision and the drive to win, there is no reason for an organisation to suffer the work involved in clarifying strategy. If an organisation is not clear about where it's going, there's no need to advertise the fact. Everybody notices soon enough.

The death of strategy is to get it mixed up with budgets. I am continually dismayed by managers' devotion to budgets. Budgets are coffins. Beginning in August, certainly by November, the number of man-hours wasted on detailed budgets for the following year is frightening. They encourage micro-management, even by enlightened managers. They are the death of the long view. What is needed instead, in broad brush-strokes, is the financial envelope within which the company must operate. The purchase of paper-clips can be dealt with at the appropriate level.

Budgets hi-jack the time available to discuss the really important strategic issues. The result is that strategy is discussed, if at all, in a bitty fashion. A good strategy is a comprehensive strategy. An incomplete strategy can lead to bad surprises.

I have endeavoured to outline the questions that need answers if we are to have a reasonably complete strategy. They are in the *Strategic Cascade* at the end of this chapter.

Strategy is the step-by-step removal of removable constraints. There is confusion between winning today's battles, which is one thing, and making tomorrow's battles winnable, which is quite another. The first question asked is, "How are we going to solve this problem?" when it should be, "Why is this problem at present insoluble?"

The purpose of being in business is to provide *distinct* products and services to customers at a value superior to those offered by competitors. Without a strategy, valuable resources are diluted, work is unfocused, and distinctiveness will not be achieved.

We don't need fortune-tellers to tell us that. And remember Brier's First Law: *At some time in the life-cycle of virtually every organisation, its ability to succeed in spite of itself runs out.* Competitive strategy is about being different. It means deliberately choosing a different set of activities to deliver a unique mix of value.

The market is the place where there is a bullet with your company's name on it. You can't dodge it. Your teflon is in being distinctive.

Distinctiveness is when a company identifies a customer's needs and either packages its product or services to meet those needs in a way superior to its competitors, or introduces a new product or service to meet needs that customers did not know existed. Customers' needs may disappear because customers change or because a competitor finds a better way to meet those needs. Will Rogers said, "Even if you're on the right track, you'll get run over if you just sit there".

Strategy is about managing change and reducing uncertainty. (You can never *eliminate* uncertainty.) At this stage in the historical development of management "science", we do really know how we get from A to B.

We *know* that autocracy does not work over the long term. We *know* that, in innovative organisations, there will be a need for greater involvement with the job as an experience in itself, instead of as a burden tolerated for future promotion or reward.

We *know* that there will be a desire for greater collegiality, for teamwork, that there will be an increase in assertiveness and a diminution in deference — people don't say "Sir" any more.

We *know* there will be a demand for management to demonstrate competence and co-operation, rather than to depend on hierarchic authority.

But we also know what St. Paul wrote to the Romans: "For the good that I would I do not: but the evil which I would not, that I do". Or, what Ovid said in the *Metamorphoses*: "I see the better things, and approve; I follow the worse".

Matthew Arnold finished the quatrain:

We do not what we ought;

What we ought not, we do;

And lean upon the thought

That chance will bring us through.

Sure – chance, luck, circumstance play a part — but getting from A to B needs teamwork, creativity, originality, inventiveness, intuition, imagination and courage, none of them capable of measurement and none of them responsive to compulsion.

THE STRATEGIC CASCADE

→ **Environment**	Rapid and continuous change – social, political, technological, commercial, values. Do we really know/understand what's going on?
→ **Vision**	What do we aspire to? What inspires us?
→ **Mission**	What business are we in? What is our unique legitimacy, our USP? Where are we going?
→ **Strategy**	How do we get there? What are the obstacles? How do we overcome them?
→ **Structure**	What is the best way to organise/distribute power and work? What kind of engine/structure do we need to overcome obstacles, to get things done?
→ **People**	What kind of attitudes, skills, knowledge,, energy and motivation do we need? Do we have them now? Do we develop and reward people appropriately?
→ **Standards**	Against what criteria/benchmarks do we continually measure ourselves?
→ **Control**	How do we know when we're off course or need to change direction? Do we have accurate and comprehensive information freely and continually communicated?
→ **Leadership**	What kind of leadership will make all this happen? Do we have it?

Entry to the process is interactive / at any point / not sequential

15

THE FALLACY OF COMPULSION

How to persuade people at work to volunteer their minds and energies to purposes they consider worthwhile is our most important strategic problem.

Compulsion always breaks down in practice. It is practicable to prevent people doing something. It is not possible to make people do something without risking more than is gained from the compelled effort.

Efficiency springs from enthusiasm. Enthusiasm is incompatible with compulsion — because it is essentially spontaneous. If, when I die, I am remembered by somebody for just one equation, I hope it would be *enthusiasm = efficiency*. Compulsion is bound to deaden enthusiasm — because it dries up the source.

True consent can be gained only by persuasion. Enduring enthusiasm can be gained only by participation.

An impatient manager may be attracted to compulsion. This is like responding to a complex social problem by saying, "There ought to be a law about it". Laws are there to stop the bad guys. "He who will live by precept will be without the habit of honesty" (John Donne).

How to persuade people at work to volunteer their minds and energies to purposes they consider worthwhile may be our most important strategic problem in the future.

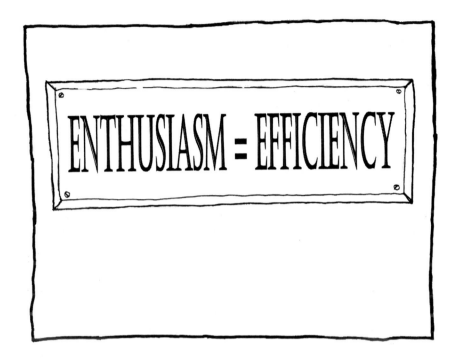

When people lose sight of their work, when they become insecure as a result of poor leadership, or when they are asked to do what they are not capable of doing and must endure the humiliation of poor performance, they turn to politics. The lesson they learn is how to be manipulative and devious. Work becomes detached from authority and there is a consequent encouragement of irrationality, of politicking.

The job of the manager is to keep politics out and substance in.

Substance is making and selling products and services. The purpose of business is to add value for customers, to create work for employees, to make a profit for shareholders, and, in doing all these things, to survive. That takes talent, and talent must focus primarily on substance. Organisational adroitness is important but it is secondary to figuring out what people want and creating the products that will succeed in the marketplace. (In politics the order is reversed: organisational adroitness comes first — getting and retaining power is more important than what is done with that power.)

You can't make every job in the organisation fit the aspirations of every individual even at the best of times. There will always be people who either won't or can't adapt — and with whom the organisation must part company. It is better to replace them lest their misery becomes infectious.

I have spent many years tinkering with the workings of organisations large and small in the hope of making things happen despite the people ensconced in them.

Constant frustration has led me to conclude that it is always better to go for the people — that is, to remove those who will never have the wit, strength of character or motivation to shoulder the burden of change, and to replace them with better men and women. What divides sheep from goats is easier to sense than to describe, which probably means that it derives from the primal core of personality. And I do not believe the primal core of personality can be changed — no matter what you do.

16

OPPORTUNITY IS BALD BEHIND

The leadership of change is not for the faint-hearted. One of the greatest barriers is lack of cohesion in the top team.

Rabelais said, "Opportunity has only a forelock: once it has passed you by, nothing you can do will bring it back, it is bald behind and never again turns its head". John Jefferson Smurfit, founder of the Smurfit Group, said, "Opportunity comes to pass, not to pause".

Revitalising an organisation that has come adrift may well require the entrepreneurial spirit that was in every successful organisation in its infancy. What distinguishes entrepreneurs from ordinary mortals is that they are the ones *who see the opportunities and do something about them*. They see beyond present boundaries to new possibilities. They are alert and disciplined and concentrate only on the best opportunities, not exhausting themselves chasing every option. They are active and focused and use every help available. They are able to infuse mature companies with a new vision and to transform them.

They do this by changing the way management sees both the company itself and the world in which it operates and then by exposing the organisation's (genuine) strengths and weaknesses to the new reality.

Corporate visions emerge slowly. They form progressively a settled core of beliefs that then go unchallenged. By changing the

company's vision of itself and of its context, new energy is set
free.

The essential first act is to consolidate the key leadership group
behind the new vision. This is not always easy. The group who
report directly to the chief executive will have their fiefdoms
which they will jealously guard. Lack of cohesion in the top team
is one of the greatest barriers to change. I have seen chief
executives who were afraid to push their barons too hard lest they
lose their allegiance. Allegiance is not much good if it is pointed
in the wrong direction. The leadership of change is not for the
faint-hearted.

A leader, as we said, cannot function without followers. A
leader's job is to transform the company, not to replace it.
Certainly he can take specific decisions to sell parts of the
portfolio and add others. Short of liquidating the lot, the core will
remain and need renewal. But nothing much will happen until his
vision is shared by his followers.

17

MANAGING CHANGE

Job protection is at the root of all resistance to change.

Faced with change, the first question to strike people is, "How does it affect me?" People do not resist change. They resist loss. Individuals resist when they are *insecure*:

- When they are uncertain about the nature and impact of the change
- When they are called on to take risks they do not like
- When they feel incompetent to perform a new role
- When they are incapable and/or unwilling to learn new skills and behaviour
- When they feel the change might make them redundant.

Individuals also resist when *their position is threatened*:

- When they expect their share of rewards to be reduced
- When they feel the change will lessen their authority over decisions
- When it lessens their control over resources
- When it lessens their personal prestige and reputation.

Tony Eccles of the London Business School has suggested a hierarchy of techniques to overcome resistance, ranging from persuasion, through bribery and flattery, to firing people who remain nuisances. He cites the example of a British health minister who, when asked how he would get the support of complaining medical consultants for the National Health Service, said, "We will stuff their mouths with gold." And it worked.

I have learned two lessons:

- The first is that at the bottom of all resistance to change is an understandable motivation: job protection.

- The second is that the only enduring way to change an individual is to give him or her something different to do.

Many efforts to change an organisation fail because they miss the target.

There are three key elements in an individual's participation in an organisation: work, relationships, rewards.

Work is what an individual *does*; the way in which he or she produces outputs, adds value, reaches results. *Relationships* are with superiors, subordinates, peers; also, in a more unspecified way, with "the organisation". *Rewards* are what an individual is paid, the status accorded, the appreciation of effort, the opportunities for promotion.

The difference between work, on the one hand, and relationships and rewards, on the other, is critical. Work can give intrinsic motivation. The motivation from relationships and rewards is extrinsic. The motivation from work can be enduring. The motivation from relationships and rewards is episodic — "eaten bread is soon forgotten". Work *can* give *continuous* learning, identity, security and growth. Rewards and relationships cannot. Work can be an enduring motivator. Relationships and rewards are episodic motivators.

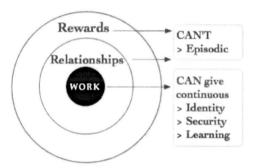

If people are suited to the work they do, and find it satisfying in itself, they *can* have that satisfaction ruined by an unpleasant boss, by peer jealousy, or by not being paid enough. If people are *not* suited to the work they do, and do not enjoy it for itself, the warmest personal relationships and the most generous rewards *cannot* make them enjoy it, *cannot* make them do it well, at least over any sustained period. They end up, as Hertzberg said, being unhappy in a greater degree of comfort.

An analogy helps to illustrate. In playing a game, there are two objectives: enjoyment of the game itself, and winning. The game itself is what causes people to choose golf instead of sailing or soccer. It is what gives them the intrinsic satisfaction. Since games are competitive, it is also nice to win. If people lost every game they played, they would give up. On the other hand, their essential objective is not an infinite series of victories. Victories or defeats are, in fact, indicators of whether the essential objective of enjoying the game is being attained.

I have been preaching this little homily for long enough to know the danger of being misunderstood. I have heard people say, "That fellow doesn't think money is important". Contrary to popular belief, I am not that daft. Of course, money is important, particularly if you don't have enough. Of course, relationships are important, particularly if your boss is making life a misery.

I sat in on an interview where an unhappy employee came to see the chief executive. He was trying to explain to his boss that he was getting no satisfaction from his work.

The boss said, "John, what on earth is wrong with you? You're well paid. You have a job for life. Everybody here likes you and I'd trust you with my life. For goodness' sake, man, count your blessings".

The employee departed in a cloud of gloom, knowing that he had failed to communicate the heart of the matter. When he had left, the boss threw his eyes up to heaven and said to me, "How can you deal with unreasonable people like that?".

The chief executive, a kindly man, was responding as many organisations do, trying to solve problems at the periphery rather than at the centre and, by so doing, unconsciously encouraging conformity and dependence.

In the past 20 years, I have worked with more than a thousand managers who spoke openly in conditions of total confidentiality. I have found that at least one-third of them lived lives, if not of quiet desperation, at least of quiet unhappiness.

The result was that the organisations to which they belonged were firing on four out of six cylinders. Those organisations were slower, less responsive, than they might have been.

You won't get change simply by being nice to people or paying them more. The heart of the matter is what they do. Change that and you change the people: their purpose, their skills, their attitudes. Change the people and you change the organisation. *Then* the rewards follow.

Giving people something different to do in a new context *forces* change.

18

ORGANISATION STRUCTURE: A CLASSIC EITHER/OR

Organisation structures are human artefacts.
They can liberate or strangle.

"We tend to meet any new situation by reorganising and a wonderful method it can be for creating the illusion of progress while producing inefficiency and demoralisation", said Petronius in the first century.

When I worked in the Irish Management Institute, which had a kind of matrix structure, new recruits would ask me about our organisation chart. I told them the best thing they could do was to take a blank sheet of paper, put themselves in the middle of it, and draw lines to the other people with whom they had a meaningful relationship.

I hesitated to write anything at all about organisation structure — for two reasons: first, because it is an area of management in which insights are developing exponentially; secondly, because, in my own work with companies, I have found it a most difficult area to tackle.

Drawing an organisation chart with straight lines and dotted lines, with levels and boxes, can afford endless hours of enjoyment.

Putting people in the boxes can cause hell to break loose. We said the barrier to change is job protection. Try putting someone on a chart at a level lower than they expect and you will be in for a painful interview.

The basic organisation model in most companies comes from Alfred Sloan and General Motors in the 1920s: a decentralised manufacturing system with centralised policy and financial control.

Our devotion to 80-year-old structures is not confined to business.[6] Tom Barrington said of Irish government that: "At base, there is the blind adherence, individually and collectively, administratively and politically, to the management methods of the small farm and the village shop".

Because we cannot see beyond the old structures and, therefore, are unlikely to change or experiment, we treat structures as static and we see different structural options as mutually exclusive.

Strategy is knowing what you want to do, and organisation is knowing how to do it. Since you have to know what it is you want to do before you can know how to do it, *organisation always lags behind strategy*.

No structure can ever be totally appropriate to carry out a firm's strategy. It is always trying to catch up. And there is Catch-22. When you get there, "there" is not there any more, because strategy is always focused on the future and we cannot *know* the future. Structure, on the other hand, is rooted in the past/present which we do know. Structures can be created for businesses that are going out of existence.

If strategies are built around life-cycles, if structures are built around strategies, and if we don't want structures to lag behind the purposes for which they were created, then we need to build in the time dimension. We can begin by asking, "Given the kind of business our strategy tells us we intend to be, what is the appropriate structure for *that business*? How does it differ from the

---

6   "The machine-age principles, although familiar and enduring, often quietly facilitate the stagnation and decline of traditional enterprises that are faced with discontinuous change." Richard T Pascale and others (2000), *Surfing the Edge of Chaos*, London: Texere (*Highly recommended*: ISBN 1 58799 064 4).

current structure? What steps are necessary to move it from here to there?"

A business can be structured around:

- The things that it does — functions
- What it makes or provides — products or services
- The places that it does those things — geography
- And/or the people it does these for — markets.

These structural elements were arranged, *one at a time*, according to a pecking order of importance. The interrelationship of the structural parts was *sequential*, not simultaneous. For example, you could not give equal primacy to both function and product. You could not have your cake and eat it. Contrary to what we have been arguing throughout this book, it was always either/or. The result was that, in solving one organisational problem, we created another.

For example, the basic benefits of centralisation are integration and control. The main benefits of decentralisation are specialisation, flexibility, autonomy, and the ability to make decisions close to the marketplace. I don't know any managers who would not want to give more freedom to their subordinates — so long as they don't lose control in the process. And I also don't know any managers who don't want as much control as they can get — so long as it does not limit everyone's flexibility and ability to deliver.

Some years ago, Ireland's most troublesome state company, CIE — road and rail transport — would employ consultants to tell them they should be decentralised. After a time, they would employ consultants to tell them they should be centralised. The consultants' reports came to be known as the Dead CIE Scrolls.

Structure at its worst can be a turbid collection of vested interests. Here are a few lessons learned:

1. Participative management can take structural change only so far. It is one area where the ultimate decision must be taken surgically, autocratically, and with a clear strategy in view: no bolt-holes, no escape hatches. Otherwise the discussion will be circular and leaky.

2. Organisation structures are human artefacts. They are *always* imperfect. They face continuous and unpredictable change. They therefore require continuous review and continuous change/development.

3. This is hard for some people, intellectually and morally. Sensitivity is needed, but ultimately you may have to go back to lesson 1.

4. Good managers know instinctively when a structure does not fit changing needs. Trust your instinct and *act* on it. It can be exhilarating. Suppressing your true instinct causes enduring frustration. All managers remember important decisions based on intuition that turned out to be right. And they remember times when they went against their better judgment and things turned out wrong.

5. And, in all of this, avoid the traps of false dichotomies or of applying simple solutions to complex organisation problems. The tentacles of structure reach deep into every organisation. They can liberate or strangle.

19

HOW DO MANAGERS LEARN?

Managers learn from other managers trying to solve problems.

If organisation structures lag behind strategy, then capability lags behind structure. Capability can be defined as the range of management knowledge, energy, experience and creativity available at any given time for present and future tasks. Hamel and Prahalad said that, when you conceive of a company as a portfolio of competencies, a whole new range of potential opportunities opens up.

In my experience, few companies do that. Few enough companies take human resources (a horrible phrase) really seriously — certainly not so seriously as they take "hard" management functions, marketing, production or finance. Human resources departments, *aka* personnel management, usually get the hind tit. At best they are seen as a bit soft, i.e., not capable of delivering immediate tangible results; at worst as tea-and-sympathy, a shoulder for disgruntled employees — until, of course, the unions get stroppy, then it's HR's fault. "People are our most important asset" has caused more cynicism than any other management slogan.

How do managers learn? Managers learn from other managers trying to solve problems. Management/capability development is about harnessing, as best we can, the manager's natural tendency to learn from his or her own messy experience.

The most influential person in this process is the manager's boss. There's an old army saying that, when you're a corporal, the world is full of sergeants, and, when you're a colonel, the world is full of generals.

Contrary to the Peter Principle, you do not have to be promoted to reach the level of your incompetence. Managers who have performed their old job well may find themselves unable to cope with growing complexity. Though they remain in the same nominal job, the demands made on that job may change. Though they may have been competent in that job until then, they find themselves incompetent from then on.

It's not easy to encourage management/capability development because the outcome cannot be predicted precisely. You have seen managers perform brilliantly in one set of circumstances only to fail in a different situation. Useful management/capability development is threatening. Real problems — not "case studies" — can cover you with glory or with egg. If they don't have both potentials, they aren't real problems, and learning, if there is any, is limited. Case studies give neither wisdom nor experience.

Management/capability development begins with the quality of the recruitment process. Use the people — you will know them — who have a genius for character judgment. They may or may not know how or why they have it but it doesn't matter. Mistaken appointments and promotions cost a fortune in the end.

And don't send people on training courses unless there is a clear-cut case for the application to a specific problem area of a new method or technique. Instead, help people to understand what goes on, in messy reality, all around them. This calls for more skill and intelligence than "training".

Above all, try to think of your colleagues with some affection and regard. Real talent almost invariably comes in awkward packages, because good managers are always irritated by the imperfections of the enterprise.

Management/capability development, the growth of managers in attitudes, skills and knowledge, is *not* the responsibility of the HR department. It is the responsibility of every manager in the organisation, from the CEO down. Serious development of human potential requires dedicated leadership, remorseless commitment, professionalism and, above all, continuing measurement of individual managers, for many of whom a change in personal priorities may be essential.

It is said that what gets measured gets done. Conversely what is not measured remains an aspiration, pious or not.

Management/capability development is not an end in itself.

There is always a gap between the aspirations of a growing organisation and its capability. The job is to *narrow the gap*. And for one reason only: competitive advantage. It's no good having grand visions and great expectations if you can't *do* them or do them well.

20

UNFINISHED BUSINESS

"It's not what's ahead — today is the golden time."

This short book has to end somewhere. Paul Valéry said, *"Un poème n'est jamais achevé — c'est toujours un accident qui le termine, c'est-à-dire qui le donne au public"*. "A poem is never finished; it's always an accident that puts a stop to it — that is to say, gives it to the public".

A colleague in Trinity College Dublin said to me, "When you've written something, stop picking at it, publish it and go on and write something else".

The book is short and the chapters shorter because it is addressed to practising managers. Managers' principal concern is *doing*, getting on with the job. Most of them are worldly-wise and tolerant. The best of them have an instinctive wisdom. A number of them indulge in bad or conspicuous behaviour but usually get found out: management depends on results, not nastiness or flimflam.

But few of them have the time (or the inclination) to read long books. They *buy* books as a result of word-of-mouth, or from a good review in a business magazine, or from boredom at an airport, but, more often than not, they don't get far past the dust-jacket.

And they are as affected as all of us are by the dumbing down of the soundbite society. I can remember a time when the fallaciousness of the *ad hominem* argument was so obvious that you would be embarrassed to use it. No longer.

Even if we continue to assume that we are dealing with intelligent people, we can't believe they are acting on an impulse to find the truth. What we have increasingly are ideologists who assess the truth, not by its concordance with reality, but by its concordance with psychological and ideological needs. Whether incompetence or deceitfulness is to blame is neither here nor there. The result itself is both incompetent and deceitful.

The title of this last note has to be an oxymoron. "Business" is never finished. In any event, we said that management was all about an unknowable future. Part of what keeps managers going is a belief that there is light at the end of the tunnel. I make a point of asking the searching question, "How's business?" The answer invariably is, "Next year will be difficult, but after that we should be all right".

So my final piece of advice comes from the late Tom Roche, one of the best Irish business leaders, *via* Jimmy Sheehan, one of the best Irish entrepreneurs, "It's not what's ahead — today is the golden time".

If you would like to read on, in the following pages we discuss some barriers in the search for truth.

21

AFTERTHOUGHT:
BRIARS AND BRAMBLES —
BARRIERS TO TRUTH

Only a man who has himself gone in search of truth knows how deceptive is the blaze of evidence with which a proposition may suddenly dazzle his eyes. The light soon fails, and the hunt is on again.
Bertrand de Jouvenel

Aquinas's definition of truth was adaequatio intellectus et rei, *i.e., an exact correspondence between perception and reality. However, we only know something within given horizons. Hence all human knowledge of truth is one-sided. No human statement can be taken as definitive. The disclosure of truth is a process of dialogue.[7]*

There's the old story of the professor of medicine at Edinburgh University. Addressing a class of young medical graduates, he said, "I have to tell ye, half of what ye've learned is not true. The trouble is I don't know which half that is".

Blaise Pascal said: "There are truths on this side of the Pyrenees that are falsehoods on the other".

In casual conversation with the poet, Brendan Kennelly, we pondered what the problem with writing was. I said, "Getting it

---

[7]   See Karl Rahner and others, eds. (1970), *Sacramentum Mundi,* New York: Herder and Herder, Vol. 6.

right". He said, "Do you know what sin is? Getting it wrong". Kennelly's words stuck and I put under academic discipline the manuscript for a book, *Freedom and Order*, together with other published material stretching back to 1960. It was a punishing experience — not remotely caused by my internal examiner, Dr. Richard Teare in Oxford, nor by my extern, Professor Tony Cunningham in Dublin. The punishment was self-inflicted. I found an unsettling piece of intellectual cosiness. I had studied over the years those works that reinforced my beliefs and scanned dismissively those that disturbed them. We tend to filter out or to ignore or to forget the less pleasant bits of reality, but the fact that everybody is at it does not make sin — getting it wrong— less sinful.

"What I have written, I have written", said Pontius Pilate. I have had the effrontery to write this book because I believe what's in it is true. I believe it's true because it has been tested in practice.

A good manager's best quality is common sense. There are put-downs of common sense — that it is none too common and that it does not make much sense. I have high respect for the many writers who raise our eyes above our shallow horizons. I have equally high respect for the pure stream of common sense that flows in every organisation I have worked with. Again and again, managers have said to me, "It's not rocket science". Peter Drucker would agree. Sure, there are briars and brambles that impede and obscure the stream.

WHAT IS TRUTH?

What is truth?" asked Pontius Pilate. What would your answer be? You might find it easier to answer the question, "What is untruth? What is a lie?" Because you *know* certain things are *untrue*. But truth is a somewhat slipperier concept.

Can you ever be sure that what you hear — or, more important, what you say — is true? Absolutely true?

In affairs, in management, in organisations, in business, there are no absolute truths. "Don't bring me the good facts", said Tony

O'Reilly. "Don't bring me the bad facts. Bring me all the facts. Facts are friendly".

The nearest we can come to truth is consensus, defined, for our purpose, as people seeing the same things from different angles.

Long ago, in the deep forests of Ireland, there was a great chieftain who was both loved and feared by his followers. One day, as he was sitting discussing strategy with his barons, a wood-carver brought him a gift — a beautifully carved bird. He held it up so that his barons could admire it and said, "Look, my friends, what a beautiful eagle", because he thought that only an eagle would be a fitting tribute to a great chieftain such as he.

He was a little disappointed at the lack of reaction from the barons. He said, "Well, it is an eagle, isn't it?" A few of the smaller barons nodded vigorously.

So he called in his counsellor, a wise and trusted man, and asked him, "Counsellor, what do you say this carving is?"

The counsellor said, "Sir, I have only my own opinion but, if you will allow me, I shall ask each baron in turn".

"That seems a good idea", said the chieftain.

The counsellor went round the great table, listened quietly to each baron, came back and bowed to the chieftain.

The chieftain said, "Is it not an eagle?"

The counsellor said, "I don't think so, sir. But I can tell you what your barons think".

"Well, what *do* they think?" asked the chieftain. "They think it's a sparrow, sir."

"And what do you think now, wise counsellor?" "It's definitely a sparrow, sir", said the counsellor.

The chieftain was faced with a choice. He felt his authority was being questioned. He could say, "Gentlemen, it's an eagle — because I say it is, and that's final". Or he could say, "Gentlemen, I value your advice. There is high consensus among you. It's a sparrow".

Being a great chieftain, he took the wiser choice and the barons became a team.

What the chieftain realised was that *the more you understand present reality, the more confidently you can move into the future.*

DEPENDENCIES

Take a scene in the life of what used to be the traditional family, where the husband went out to work and the wife stayed home to mind the two or three children.

The husband appears home, white-faced. His wife senses that something is badly wrong. The kids give a cheery chorus of "Hi Dad!" and are ignored. The husband asks his wife to come into the living room and to close the door. He sits with his head in his hands and tells her, "I've been fired".

It is an unambiguous message. What is her immediate reaction? Does she take him in her arms and say, "You poor thing"? Does she say, "Here. Let me get you a drink"? Possibly — if she's of heroic disposition. More likely her instinctive reaction will be, "My God, what's going to happen to me and the kids?".

She is *dependent* on her husband. The wife hears not primarily the message that her husband has been fired: that message is drowned in a wave of concern for herself and her children. It has been radically altered from its original intent. What the wife hears is refracted by her dependency.

If dependency is a characteristic of that nucleus of organised life, the family, a unit bonded by love, how much more so is it a characteristic of work organisations, bonded by necessity?

"We're all in this together" is whimsical organisation folklore. It is at the same level of comforting daftness as the phrase "social partners", used by politicians on ritual occasions when they have to talk to both sides at once and are stuck for something to say.

What you see depends on where you stand. What you say depends on who you're speaking to.

A colleague, Professor Theodore Weinshall of the University of Tel-Aviv, has proved that, for every level in an organisation through which information passes, it may lose up to half its meaning.

People in organisations withhold from one another what they think and feel about what really goes on. They are never completely frank about the direction the organisation is going in, about the pressures from competing enterprises, about the way decisions are made or the style of leadership, about the way resources are allocated or who are the favourite sons.

People worry about what their boss thinks of them. They worry about their peers with whom they compete for the favour of a common superior. They worry about their subordinates, younger and more recently educated, whose acquired knowledge of the organisation may soon rival their own.

Consequently, they never fully open up. They communicate only part of their inner truth and part of what they communicate is the opposite of their real thoughts and feelings. The result is that organisations can exist in a twilight where reality may never be fully visible.

Organisations and individuals are prisoners of their dependencies. Which brings us back to Pontius Pilate's question.

How could we ever do justice to the words used in court: "The truth, the whole truth and nothing but the truth"? They mock our clumsy efforts even to remember and to convey our experiences, never mind overcoming the barriers created by dependencies.

MEDIATORS

There is a further barrier to truth: the fact that much of what is inside our heads is *mediated*. There is a line in Tom Stoppard's play, *Jumpers*: "The media. It sounds like a convention of spiritualists". While the word is relatively recent and carries a whiff of disparagement, it is not a bad one to describe the intermediaries between us and our information.

Some years ago, I saw the late Cardinal Basil Hume interviewed on BBC television. The smug interviewer built up to his question with a long preamble, peppered with "Some people would say". When finally he stopped, the Cardinal looked at him brightly and answered, "Who told you that?".

In the news media, content moves along a spectrum. At one end is *news, what* happened and *who* did it. Then there is *analysis, how* and *why* things happened and what their consequences might be. Finally, there is *comment*, which is what *I think* about what happened or about the issues of the day and, perhaps, what should be done about them. The distinctions along the spectrum are imperfect.

But add to them the constant need to please the market and the picture gets blurry. Lay three or four newspapers side-by-side on a day when there is not an overwhelming story. You will see an interaction between what the editor thinks is important and what the editor thinks his readers think is important. It is his choice, but it is hardly a moral one. It is not a stark choice between truthfulness and deception. It comes nearer the view of an eminent physician: "Far older than the precept, 'The truth, the whole truth, and nothing but the truth', is another that has always been the guide of best physicians: 'So far as possible, do no harm'. You can do harm by the process that is quaintly called telling the truth. You can do harm by lying. But try to do as little harm as possible".

Janus-like, the media face two ways: telling the truth and pleasing their market. There is no getting away from that latter dependency. It will not be denied by lofty arguments about journalistic standards, or taste, or vulgarity — that is simply to shift the argument onto other ground and, in any event, my standards may not be yours. The media, like the rest of us, are impure and imperfect. They too see through a glass, darkly.

The whole truth is out of reach in the media, in work organisations, even in the family.

Few of us are Yeats's swift, indifferent men: we like to please, to be thought well of, to avoid hurt, to make a few bucks, to have a quiet life, to stay inside our intellectual comfort zones. If that involves being economical with the truth, ho-hum.

Add to these constraints the awareness that everything in life connects, that all is a seamless web so that nothing can be said without qualifications and elaborations in infinite regress, and a sense of lassitude could steal over the most intrepid.

Nietzsche was taking things to their ultimate, as he usually did, when he said, "There is only *one* world, and that world is false, cruel, contradictory, misleading, senseless. We need lies to vanquish this reality, this 'truth', we need lies in order to live. That lying is a necessity of life is itself a part of the terrifying and problematic character of existence".

I quote Nietzsche to provoke, not least from myself, the response, "Things are not *that* bad", to cheer myself up and to restore that essential *balance* we mentioned earlier.

(I am *not* saying, "I am, however, optimistic", a phrase beloved of politicians and which, in their exquisite desire to please, they use at the end of a doom-laden peroration, undoing all that has gone before.)

I believe we shall keep that necessary balance so long as we are aware that life is paradox: a continual compromise between good and evil, between truth and untruth, between light and shade.

Compromise is not a heroic word. It has none of the rock-like certainty of fundamentalism, of jihad, of "No surrender!".

Uncertainty, the necessity of imperfect choice, can cause discomfort. We like fixed things. If pushed, we can raise them to the level of "principles".

"Sticking to our principles", if it is merely an unwillingness to face uncertainty, paradox or personal discomfort, is about as sensible as being against the use of electricity.

FOOLISH NOTIONS

"Principles" can be laden with nostalgia. Karl Marx said, "The tradition of all the dead generations weighs like a nightmare on the brain of the living". It is hard to slough off the dead, though still protective, tissue of old attitudes and behaviour and dependencies, of old certainties.

Since we can so seldom *find* it, since there are so many barriers, what is needed is a constant *search* for truth. This means *constant* questioning and *constant* experimentation. It requires radicalism — the opposite of wishful thinking. It calls for analytical staying power, a determination to keep asking why. Radicalism is the art of the necessary.

It requires us to break free from the womb of either/or thinking, to work in the knowledge that we are beset not by stark choices, but by continual paradoxes — and to recognise that, year upon year, we may have been laying down layer upon layer of protective tissue.

The message is time-worn and difficult: *never believe your own propaganda*. In other words, it might help if we applied to our own lapidary utterances the same astringent eye we apply to the pomposities of others.

Since none of us can ever possess the whole truth, it might help if we listened to those who disagree with us and occasionally committed the indiscretion of changing our minds.

We remember:

> *O wad some Pow'r the giftie gie us*
> *To see ourselves as others see us!*

But do we remember the punch line?

> *It wad from many a blunder free us,*
> *And foolish notion.*

If we always keep a-hold of Nurse, for fear of finding something worse, we could end up like the man in Maurice Evan Hare's limerick:

> *There once was a man who said, "Damn!*
> *It is borne in upon me I am*
> *An engine that moves*
> *In predestinate grooves*
> *I'm not even a bus, I'm a tram".*

FREEDOM AND ORDER

Do you remember Einstein's definition of insanity? *Endlessly repeating the same process hoping for a different outcome.*

Why is it that, when change is happening all around us, most of our organisations are still run like the old Soviet Gosplan — on tram-tracks? A bit like the Victorian six-to-a-bed — when father says "Turn", we all turn.

Faced with change, we need two things. We need freedom and we need order.

Without freedom, you get recidivist organisations. Without order, you get anarchy.

In our market or mixed economy, people are free to make their own decisions within a known framework established by law. This framework is based on the conviction that there is an inherent benefit to the individuals in our society in favouring the free as against the authoritarian way of doing things. This is a form deeply rooted in the worth of the individual. To us, the individual — not a class or a state or an organisation — is the central element. The individual's consent is the essence of our political life. The individual's happiness is the essence of our economic philosophy. The individual's salvation is the essence of our spiritual order. The individual's freedom is the ultimate test of all we value.

Freedom is not licence; nor is it libertarianism; nor a modish liberalism. It was not even as an element in the happiness of the individual that, throughout history, lofty spirits vaunted freedom. It was because freedom consecrated the dignity of the human personality. Freedom saved the individual from playing the merely instrumental role to which authority always tends to reduce people.

Those laws are best that require least reinforcement: laws that are rooted in the moral habits of the citizens and enjoy their respect. We need to distinguish between laws and commands. Laws are impersonal rules, general, disinterested, usually negative in form: "Thou shalt not kill". Laws are observed. Commands are obeyed. To live under the rule of law is to be a citizen. To live under commandment is to be a subject.

If freedom is so fundamental to us, is it not reasonable to suggest that the organisations that maximise individual freedom will be the effective ones, flexible, responsive at a time of change? And is it not equally reasonable to suggest that organisations that encourage conformity and dependence will be dull and unresponsive to change?

This is where order comes in. With order goes personal responsibility. Order is about knowing where you stand, what is expected of you, where your organisation is going. It is about having a continuous flow of *information* — knowledge — so that you can take your own decisions within accepted limits. Order is about clarity. The opposite of clarity is ignorance, uncertainty and lack of confidence, leading to stasis, a polite word for constipation.

However, order must not be confused with bureaucracy. Bureaucracy means unnecessary rules and regulations. Reliance on bureaucracy is a sure sign of an absence of strategy. The right balance is a boundary like a chalk line on the ground rather than a stone wall. You are free to cross it, but you are also very clear where it is and what the consequences of trespass will be.

COMMUNICATING

My favourite Thurber cartoon is an eager swain saying to the object of his ardour, "What do you want to be inscrutable *for*, Marcia?"

I have never worked in an organisation that did not have communication problems. It was not so much a desire for inscrutability (though I have seen the most banal memos headed "Eyes Only"), rather it was the reluctance of managers to get out and mix it with the troops, to listen and argue, to change their mind occasionally, genuinely to share with colleagues their vision of the future.

We are living through an information revolution. It is dissonant to have expectations in our civil life greatly at variance with what we can expect in our work life.

Managers in moments of weariness may hanker after the good old days, when there was a decent privacy, when life seemed more predictable, when people did what they were told and minded their own business. God blessed the squire and his relations, and kept us in our proper stations.

It was the late Marshall McLuhan, author of *The Medium is the Massage*, who said, "You can't go home any more". It was a graffito in the restroom of New York's Grand Central Station that reminded us: "Nostalgia kills".

Whose heart does not beat a little faster at the words of the chairman of the board in a *New Yorker* cartoon:

"And though last year, as in previous years, your company had to deal with spiralling labour costs, exorbitant interest rates, and unconscionable government interference, management was able once more, through a combination of deceptive marketing practices, false advertising, and price fixing, to show a profit which, in all modesty, can only be called excessive."

Those days are gone. Anyone who relies on the past as the best guide to the future might well heed the admonition in the Preface to *The Book of Common Prayer*: "There was never anything by the wit of man so well devised, or so sure established, which in continuance of time hath not been corrupted".

Like the King, we may announce that we can repair Humpty Dumpty, but we need more horses and more men. We may try to solve problems with our existing tools in their old context, "endlessly repeating the same process".

Exact knowledge is not available in management or, for that matter, in many of the sciences bearing on human behaviour — psychology, anthropology or sociology. In these developing disciplines, it is the approach or attitude that matters. That attitude is based on a conviction that a greater *degree* of knowledge is possible, that truths are being *developed* which can be applied to practical affairs. And, beyond the point where precision is possible, problems can be handled — as they are in medicine — in the spirit of truth and with constant reference to experience.

Just as we need openness to new knowledge, we also need to remember the lessons of the past. Put the other way around: effective strategies need not squander our heritage, but they have to be unchained from those traditions, values and behaviour whose usefulness has disappeared. Talleyrand said: "In all one's actions one must have in mind the future and the past".

Anyone remember the headline years ago in an English newspaper: *Fog in the Channel — Continent Isolated*?

Or the old joke about the English that when "foreigners" did not understand, you simply shouted louder.

Or the warning to public speakers that, in any given audience, one-third are listening, one-third are dozing and one-third are having sexual fantasies.

I have seldom presented a report to a chief executive who did not exclaim, "How could they say that, when I *told* them?"

Telling is not communicating. If the pupil has not learned, the teacher has not taught. This applies also to people who write books.

ABOUT THE AUTHOR

Ivor Kenny was born in Galway in 1930, the son of a newspaper editor, founder of *The Connacht Tribune*, which recently passed successfully into its 100th year. He is married to Maureen Mac Mahon. They have five children and eight grandchildren.

He was educated at St. Ignatius College SJ; UCG; the London School of Economics; the Institut d'Etudes Politiques, Paris; and the Harvard Business School as a Fulbright Scholar.

His first job was as an announcer at the then Radio Éireann, 1955 to 1959. In 1960 he joined the staff of the Irish Management Institute and was appointed Director General in 1963. He brought the Institute from offices in a semi-detached house to the National Management Centre in Sandyford.

He retired in 1983 and was appointed Research Fellow at UCD from where he conducted consultancy assignments with international companies, including comprehensive studies for the Smurfit Group and the Kerry Group, whose boards he subsequently joined. He served on other boards, public and private, including Independent News and Media PLC and IONA Technologies Plc.

He was a Research Professor of Political Economy at Trinity College, Dublin, 1977 to 1980; Chancellor of the International Academy of Management, 1982 to 1987; Distinguished Professor of Public Policy, the International Management Centres, UK, 1983 to 2006; Professor at Cranfield University, UK, 1984; and Executive-in-Residence, Indiana University, USA, 1988.

He believes that honours and degrees should be like melting snow and that managers learn best from other managers solving real problems.

OAK TREE PRESS

Oak Tree Press develops and delivers information, advice and resources for entrepreneurs and managers. It is Ireland's leading business book publisher, with an unrivalled reputation for quality titles across business, management, HR, law, marketing and enterprise topics. NuBooks is its digital-only imprint, publishing short, focused ebooks for busy entrepreneurs and managers.

Oak Tree Press is comfortable across a range of communication media – print, web and training, focusing always on the effective communication of business information.

Oak Tree Press, 19 Rutland Street, Cork, Ireland.

T: + 353 21 4313855 F: + 353 21 4313496.

E: info@oaktreepress.com

W: www.oaktreepress.com / www.SuccessStore.com

Lightning Source UK Ltd.
Milton Keynes UK
UKOW03f0630230114

225081UK00003B/7/P